World Art Series

DEGAS/LAUTREC

by Parker Tyler/92 color plates

Doubleday & Company, Inc. Garden City, New York 1968

Library of Congress Catalog Card Number: 68-23390

First published in Japan
English-language edition first published
in Japan in September 1968
Printed in Japan

Edgar Degas

1 – *Self-portrait* 1862/Oil/92.1 x 68.9cm/National Gallery of Art, Washington D.C.
2 – *The Belleli Family* 1860-62/Oil/200.0 x 250.0cm/The Louvre, Paris
3 – *The Belleli Family (detail)*
4 – *Portrait of a Woman* 1861/Oil/41.0 x 29.0cm/Musée des Beaux-Arts, Algeria
5 – *Self-portrait* 1854-55/Oil/81.0 x 64.5cm/The Louvre, Paris
6 – *Gentlemen's Race: Before the Start* 1862/Oil/48.5 x 61.0cm/The Louvre, Paris
7 – *Start of the Chase* 1864-68/Oil/70.0 x 89.0cm/Private Collection, Paris
8 – *Portrait of a Young Woman* 1867/Oil/27.0 x 22.0cm/The Louvre, Paris
9 – *Mademoiselle Dobigny* 1869/Oil/31.0 x 26.0cm/Private Collection, Zurich
10 – *Musicians of the Orchestra* 1868-69/Oil/56.5 x 46.0cm/The Louvre, Paris
11 – *The Violoncellist Pillet* 1868-69/Oil/50.5 x 61.0cm/The Louvre, Paris
12 – *Portrait of Monsieur Ruelle* 1862/Oil/44.0 x 36.0cm/Musée des Beaux-Arts, Lyon
13 – *Race Horses: Before the Grandstand* 1869-72/Pastel/46.0 x 61.0cm/The Louvre, Paris
14 – *Madame Camus at the Piano* 1869-72/Oil/139.0 x 94.0cm/Private Collection, Zurich
15 – *Mademoiselle Dihau at the Piano* 1869-72/Oil/45.0 x 32.0cm/The Louvre, Paris
16 – *The Pedicure* 1873/Oil/61.0 x 46.0cm/The Louvre, Paris
17 – *The Man and the Puppet* 1873/Oil/41.0 x 27.0cm/National Gallery of Art, Washington D.C.
18 – *The Dancing Class* 1874/Oil/85.0 x 75.0cm/The Louvre, Paris
19 – *Ballet Rehearsal on Stage* 1874/Oil/66.0 x 82.0cm/The Louvre, Paris
20 – *At the Races: Amateur Jockeys before the Grandstand* 1877-80/Oil/66.0 x 81.0cm/The Louvre, Paris
21 – *At the Races: Amateur Jockeys before the Grandstand (detail)*
22 – *At the Ambassadeurs: Café Concert* 1876-77/Pastel/37.0 x 27.0cm/Musée des Beaux-Arts, Lyon
23 – *At the Ambassadeurs: Café Concert (detail)*
24 – *Dancer Bowing: End of an Arabesque* 1877/Pastel/67.4 x 38.0cm/The Louvre, Paris
25 – *The Star; or Dancer on Stage* 1878/Pastel/60.0 x 44.0cm/The Louvre, Paris
26 – *Dancer with Bouquet, Bowing* 1877/Pastel/75.0 x 78.0cm/The Louvre, Paris
27 – *The Ironers* 1884/Pastel/76.0 x 81.5cm/The Louvre, Paris
28 – *Injured Jockey and Bolting Horse* 1866/Oil/180.0 x 151.0cm/Private Collection, Paris
29 – *Portrait of Zacharie Zacharian* 1885/Pastel/39.0 x 39.0cm/Private Collection, Paris
30 – *After the Bath: Woman Wiping Her Feet* 1886/Pastel/54.3 x 52.4cm/The Louvre, Paris
31 – *After the Bath: Woman Wiping Her Neck* 1898/Pastel/62.2 x 65.0cm/The Louvre, Paris
32 – *Green Dancers* 1899/Pastel/Private Collection, Paris
33 – *Two Dancers* 1897/Pastel
34 – *Woman at Her Toilet* 1905-07/Pastel/77.0 x 70.0cm/Private Collection, Paris
35 – *Madame Rouart and Her Children* 1905/Pastel/160.0 x 141.0cm/Musée du Petit-Palais, Paris
36 – *Woman in the Bath* 1892/Pastel/Art Gallery of Toronto, Canada
37 – *Dancer* 1882/Bronze/The Louvre, Paris
38 – *Horse* Bronze/The Louvre, Paris
39 – *Dancer* 1882-92/Bronze/50.5cm/Bridgestone Gallery, Tokyo

Henri de Toulouse-Lautrec

40 – *Artilleryman Saddling His Horse* 1879/Oil/50.5 x 37.5cm/Musée Toulouse-Lautrec, Albi
41 – *Céleyran: View of a Vineyard* 1880/Oil/16.5 x 23.9cm/Musée Toulouse-Lautrec, Albi
42 – *Raoul Tapié of Céleyran* 1881/Oil/60.0 x 50.0cm/Private Collection, Paris
43 – *Nude Study: Woman Seated on a Divan* 1882/Oil/55.0 x 46.0cm/Musée Toulouse-Lautrec, Albi
44 – *A Laborer at Céleyran* 1882/Oil/60.0 x 42.0cm/Musée Toulouse-Lautrec, Albi
45 – *Still Life* 1882/Oil/27.0 x 22.0cm/Musée Toulouse-Lautrec, Albi
46 – *Old Woman Seated on a Bench at Céleyran* 1882/Oil/53.0 x 44.0cm/Musée Toulouse-Lautrec, Albi
47 – *La Comtesse A. de Toulouse-Lautrec* 1883/Oil/93.5 x 81.0cm/Musée Toulouse-Lautrec, Albi
48 – *The Ball at the Moulin de la Galette* 1889/Oil/90.0 x 100.0cm/Art Institute of Chicago
49 – *The Ball at the Moulin de la Galette (detail)*
50 – *The Day of First Communion* 1888/Oil/65.0 x 37.0cm/Musée des Augustins, Toulouse
51 – *At the Races* 1899/Oil/45.0 x 53.0cm/Musée Toulouse-Lautrec, Albi
52 – *At the Cirque Fernando* 1888/Oil/100.0 x 200.0cm/Art Institute of Chicago
53 – *Two Women Making Their Bed* 1889/Oil/61.0 x 80.0cm/Private Collection, Paris
54 – *Woman Curling Her Hair* 1890/Oil/55.0 x 37.0cm/Musée des Augustins, Toulouse
55 – *Gabrielle the Dancer* 1890/Oil/54.0 x 40.0cm/Musée Toulouse-Lautrec, Albi
56 – *Monsieur Désiré Dihau: Bassoonist of the Opera* 1891/Oil/55.2 x 45.0cm/Musée Toulouse-Lautrec, Albi
57 – *The Bed* 1892-95/Oil/53.0 x 70.0cm/The Louvre, Paris
58 – *Woman in Black Boa* 1892/Oil/53.0 x 41.0cm/The Louvre, Paris
59 – *The Englishman Warner at the Moulin Rouge* 1892/Lithograph/47.0 x 37.2cm/Musée Toulouse-Lautrec, Albi
60 – *Jardin de Paris: Jane Avril (after the original poster)* 1893/Lithograph/130.0 x 95.0cm/Musée de Toulouse-Lautrec, Albi
61 – *Loie Fuller at the Folies-Bergères* 1893/Oil/61.0 x 43.8cm/Musée Toulouse-Lautrec, Albi
62 – *Monsieur, Madame, and the Dog* 1893/Water Color/48.0 x 80.0cm/Musée Toulouse-Lautrec, Albi
63 – *Madame de Gortzikoff* 1893/Oil/75.0 x 51.0cm/Private Collection, London
64 – *Monsieur Louis Pascal* 1893/Oil/77.0 x 53.0cm/Musée Toulouse-Lautrec, Albi
65 – *Two Women Sitting in a Café* 1894/Crayon and Water Color/53.8 x 37.9cm/The Louvre, Paris
66 – *Woman Putting on Her Stocking* 1894/Oil/60.0 x 43.0cm/Musée Toulouse-Lautrec, Albi
67 – *Aristide Bruant* 1894/Lithograph/77.5 x 59.0cm/Musée Toulouse-Lautrec, Albi
68 – *The Tattooed Lady* 1894/Oil/62.5 x 48.0cm/Private Collection, Bern
69 – *Femme de Maison* 1894/Oil/25.2 x 19.0cm/Musée Toulouse-Lautrec, Albi
70 – *Madame Pascal at the Piano* 1895/Oil/Musée Toulouse-Lautrec, Albi
71 – *The Two Friends* 1895/Oil/65.0 x 84.0cm/Private Collection, Zurich
72 – *The Female Clown Cha-U-Kao* 1895/Oil/64.0 x 49.0cm/The Louvre, Paris
73 – *Woman at Her Toilet* 1896/Oil/67.0 x 54.0cm/The Louvre, Paris
74 – *Casual Conquest* 1896/Oil/105.0 x 67.0cm/Musée des Augustins, Toulouse
75 – *At the Café: The Guest and the Chlorotic Cashier* 1898/Oil/81.5 x 60.0cm/Kunsthaus, Zurich
76 – *Monsieur Maurice Joyant (detail)* 1900/Oil/113.0 x 79.0cm/Musée Toulouse-Lautrec, Albi
77 – *Portrait of a Woman* 1900/Oil/89.5 x 80.5cm/Ohara Art Gallery, Kurashiki, Japan
78 – *The Milliner* 1900/Oil/61.0 x 49.3cm/Musée Toulouse-Lautrec, Albi
79 – *Portrait of André Rivoire* 1901/Oil/57.5 x 46.0cm/Musée du Petit-Palais, Paris

DESSINS

Degas

Characters (after the School of Athens of Raphael)
Artist and Model
Study of Violin Player
Hair
After the Bath
Sketch of Dancer with Tambourine

Lautrec

Head of La Goulue
At the Moulin Rouge: La Goulue and La Môme Fromage
Marcelle
Napoleon I on Horseback
The Lady Clown Cha-U-Kao as Rider
Clown, Horse, and Monkey Rider
Entrance to the Track, Horse Saddled with Frame and Followed by Acrobat in Slippers
Rehearsing on the Floor
Chocolate Dancing in the Bar d'Achille

DEGAS/LAUTREC

1 Degas
Self-portrait
1862 92.1 x 68.9cm

2/3 Degas *The Belleli Family* 1860-62 200.0 x 250.0cm

4 Degas *Portrait of a Woman* 1861 41.0 x 29.0cm

5 Degas *Self Portrait* 1854-55 81.0 x 64.5cm

6 Degas *Gentlemen's Race: Before the Start* 1862 48.5 x 61.0cm

7 Degas *Start of the Chase* 1864-68 70.0 x 89.0cm

8 Degas *Portrait of a Young Woman* 1867 27.0 x 22.0cm

9 Degas *Mademoiselle Dobigny* 1869 31.0 x 26.0cm

← 10 Degas *Musicians of the Orchestra* 1868-69 56.5 x 46.0cm
11 Degas *The Violoncellist Pillet* 1868-69 50.5 x 61.0cm

12 Degas *Portrait of Monsieur Ruelle* 1862 44.0 x 36.0cm

13 Degas
Race Horses: Before the Grandstand
1869-72 46.0 x 61.0cm

14 Degas
Madame Camus at the Piano
1869-72 139.0 x 94.0cm

15 Degas *Mademoiselle Dihau at the Piano* 1869-72 45.0 x 32.5cm

16 Degas
The Pedicure
1873 61.0 x 46.0cm

17 Degas
The Man and the Puppet
1873 41.0 x 27.0cm

← 18	Degas	*The Dancing Class*	1874	85.0 x 75.0cm
19	Degas	*Ballet Rehearsal on Stage*	1874	66.0 x 82.0cm

20/21 Degas *At the Races: Amateur Jockeys before the Grandstand*
1877-80 66.0 x 81.0cm

22/23 Degas *At the Ambassadeurs: Café Concert* 1876-77 37.0 x 27.0cm

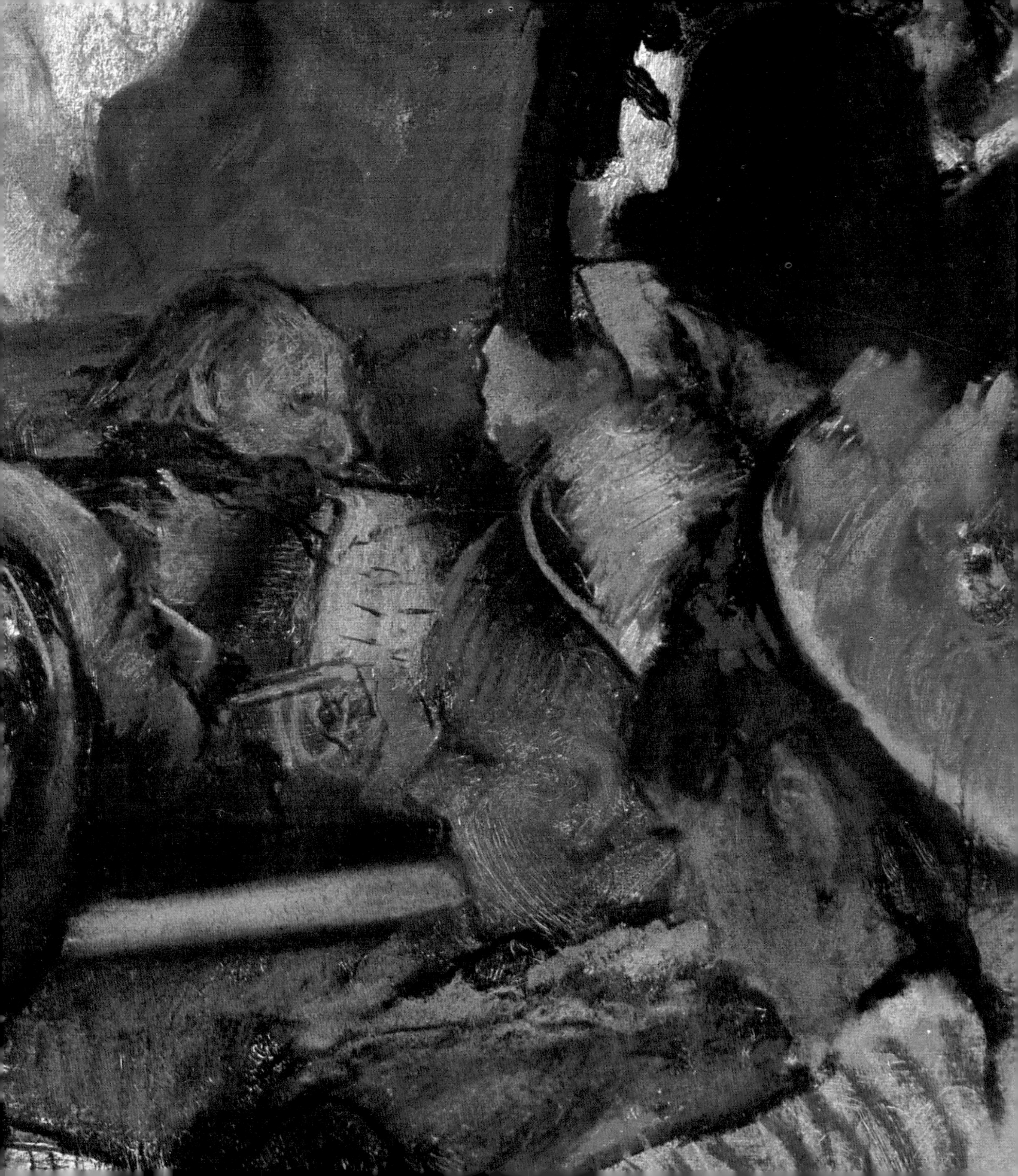

24 Degas
Dancer Bowing: End of an Arabesque
1877 67.4 x 38.0cm

25 Degas
The Star; or Dancer on Stage
1878 60.0 x 44.0cm

26 Degas *Dancer with Bouquet, Bowing* 1877 75.0 x 78.0cm

27 Degas *The Ironers* 1884 76.0 x 81.5cm

28 Degas *Injured Jockey and Bolting Horse* 1866 180.0 x 151.0cm

29 Degas *Portrait of Zacharie Zacharian* 1885 39.0 x 39.0cm

30 Degas *After the Bath: Woman Wiping Her Feet* 1886 54.3 x 52.4cm

31 Degas *After the Bath: Woman Wiping Her Neck* 1898 62.2 x 65.0cm

32 Degas *Green Dancers* 1899

33 Degas *Two Dancers* 1897

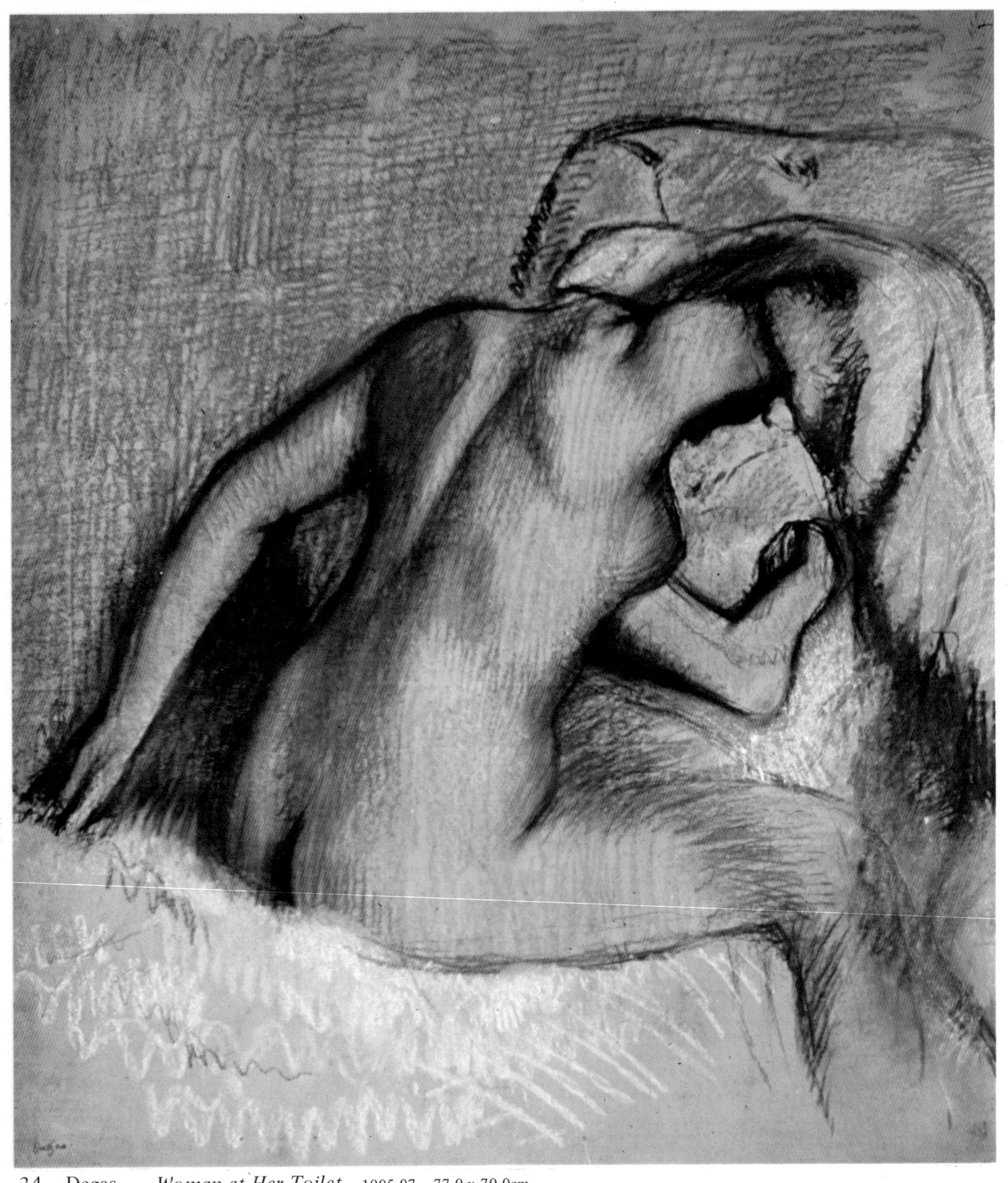

34 Degas *Woman at Her Toilet* 1905-07 77.0 x 70.0cm

35 Degas *Madame Rouart and Her Children* 1905 160.0 x 141.0cm

36 Degas *Woman in the Bath* 1892

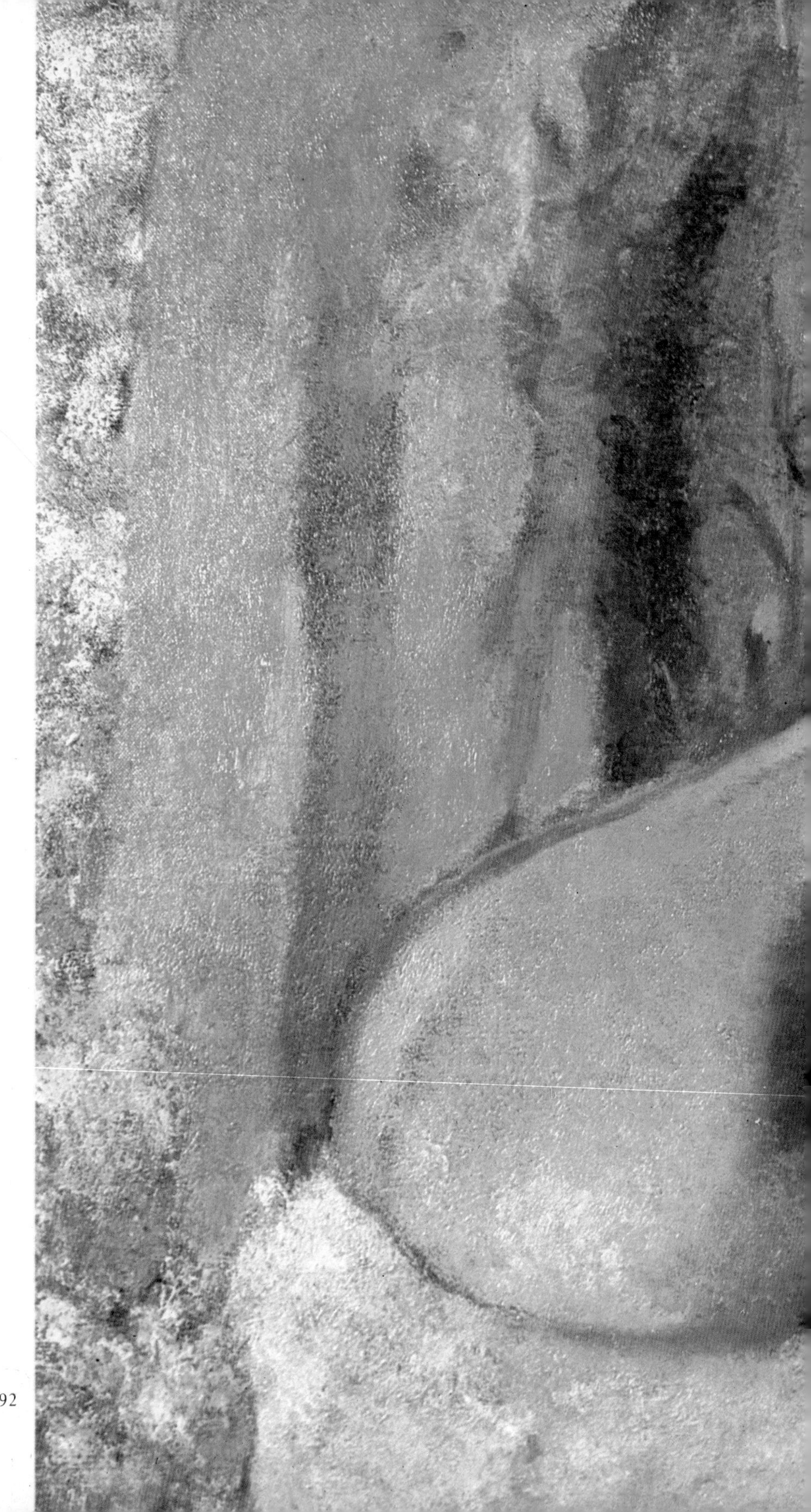

39 Degas *Dancer* 1882-92 50.5cm →

37 Degas *Dancer* 1882

38 Degas *Horse*

40 Lautrec
Artilleryman
Sadding His Horse
1879 50.5 x 37.5cm

41 Lautrec *Céleyran: View of a Vineyard* 1880 16.5 x 23.9cm

42 Lautrec *Raoul Tapié of Céleyran* 1881 60.0 x 50.0cm

43 Lautrec *Nude Study: Woman Seated on a Divan* 1882 55.0 x 46.0cm

44 Lautrec *A Laborer at Céleyran* 1882 60.0 x 42.0cm

45 Lautrec *Still Life* 1882 27.0 x 22.0cm

46 Lautrec *Old Woman Seated on a Bench at Céleyran* 1882 53.0 x 44.0cm

47 Lautrec *La Comtesse A. de Toulouse-Lautrec* 1883 93.5 x 81.0cm

48/49 Lautrec *The Ball at the Moulin de la Galette* 1889 90.0 x 100.0cm

50 Lautrec
The Day of First Communion
1888 65.0 x 37.0cm

51 Lautrec *At the Races* 1899 45.0 x 53.0cm

52 Lautrec
At the Cirque Fernando
1888 100.0 x 200.0cm

53 Lautrec *Two Women Making Their Bed* 1889 61.0 x 80.0cm

54 Lautrec
Woman Curling Her Hair
1890 55.0 x 37.0cm

55 Lautrec
Gabrielle the Dancer
1890 54.0 x 40.0cm

56 Lautrec *Monsieur Désiré Dihau: Bassoonist of the Opera* 1891 55.2 x 45.0cm

57 Lautrec *The Bed* 1892-95 53.0 x 70.0cm

58 Lautrec *Woman in Black Boa* 1892 53.0 x 41.0cm →

59 Lautrec *The Englishman Warner at the Moulin Rouge* 1892 47.0 x 37.2cm

60 Lautrec
ardin de Paris: Jane Avril
(after the original poster)
1893 130.0 x 95.0cm

61 Lautrec *Loie Full*
at the Folies-Bergères
1893 61.0 x 43.8cm

62 Lautrec *Monsieur, Madame, and the Dog* 1893 48.0 x 80.0cm

63 Lautrec
Madame de Gortzikoff
1893 75.0 x 51.0cm

64 Lautrec
Monsieur Louis Pascal
1893 77.0 x 53.0cm

65 Lautrec
Two Women Sitting in a Ca
1894 53.8 x 37.9cm

66 Lautrec
Woman Putting on Her Stocking
1894 60.0 x 43.0cm

67 Lautrec *Aristide Bruant* 1894 77.5 x 59.0cm

68 Lautrec *The Tattooed Lady* 1894 62.5 x 48.0cm

69 Lautrec
Femme de Maison
1894 25.2 x 19.0cm

70 Lautrec
Madame Pascal at the Piano 1895

71 Lautrec *The Two Friends* 1895 65.0 x 84.0cm

72 Lautrec *The Female Clown Cha-U-Kao* 1895 64.0 x 49.0cm →

← 73 Lautrec *Woman at Her Toilet*
1896 67.0 x 54.0cm

74 Lautrec *Casual Conquest*
1896 105.0 x 67.0cm

75 Lautrec *At the Café: The Guest and the Chlorotic Cashier* 1898 81.5 x 60.0cm

76 Lautrec
Monsieur Maurice Joyant
1900 113.0 x 79.0cm

77 Lautrec *Portrait of a Woman* 1900 89.5 x 80.5cm

78 Lautrec *The Milliner* 1900 61.0 x 49.3cm

79 Lautrec *Portrait of André Rivoire* 1901 57.5 x 46.0cm

DEGAS/LAUTREC

If one were to single out two painters of the nineteenth century whose works best represent the personality of the city of Paris and the more public characteristics of French urban culture, those two would inevitably be Edgar Degas and Henri de Toulouse-Lautrec. Born from his father's side into the old noble family of the Counts of Toulouse, Lautrec penetrated, nevertheless, into the more dubious, gamier levels of Parisian life, the music and dance halls, the circus, the low-life bars and the brothels, while Degas, though he too patronized brothels and painted laundresses, concentrated rather on the high theatrical culture of the Opera ballet and its orchestra. Both men, meanwhile, were also producing brilliant and memorable portraits. Together they spanned the whole fashionable, sporting, and artistic worlds of their time – horses and horse-racing forming one more subject which they had in common.

In a way, the two artists were in pronounced contrast. Born in 1834 (only four years after the senior Impressionist, Camille Pissarro), Degas, whose name was originally spelled de Gas, began practicing his art even before the year Lautrec was born, 1864, and outlived him sixteen years, lasting longer than all the Impressionists and Post-Impressionists who were substantially of his generation. The youthful Lautrec had an obsessed admiration for the exquisite painter of dancing girls, and when he held his first one-man show, Degas was the only painter whom he specifically invited to attend. Their community was the natural result of their aesthetic interests which, although in distinct senses, were largely grounded in the truth as meshed with deliberate illusion. They were characteristically modern precursors in portraying the various *theaters* of life and the paradox in the actual theater's realization of human character and motive.

Degas, about 1903

Degas's social origin had a strange parallel with that of Cézanne. He too was the son of a banker, although a more cultivated, broader-minded banker than Cézanne's father, and even at first was destined, like Cézanne, for the law. Cézanne's initiation into the art world was achieved by dint of struggle and his own personal will. The senior Degas's artistic interests, on the other hand, made going to the Louvre with his son and introducing him to great collectors of the day (at whose houses he saw the works of both old and contemporary masters) into part of the young Edgar's early education. Thus when, in 1854, Edgar Degas decided to embrace the profession of painting, his father made no objection to his studying with a follower of Ingres and entering, later, the École des Beaux-Arts.

Even as the spirit of modernity obscurely stirred in Degas, he started out in the approved academic manner by doing much copying at the Louvre and becoming a passionate devotee of Ingres. He went abroad, moreover, to study the Italian and Dutch masters of the Renaissance. Perhaps what lasted longest in his art was the finesse of portraying human features that one finds in Ingres – that is, discerning the qualities in contemporary faces that wedded them to the serene and exact balance of classical form. One may see this in Degas's self-portraits (plates 1 and 5) and in his portrait of the Belleli family (plate 2). It would not be many years, however, before Degas, like the Impressionists whose styles would be more radical, noticed how much various aspects of light could significantly transform the things on which it fell. At that period, candlelight lit both the drawing room and (in force and from a different angle) the stage. In the latter case, its way of *inundating* images, particularly from beneath, made figures on the stage the denizens of a world apart.

Degas *Studies for a Portrait of Manet*

Likewise ennobled by the Viscounts of Lautrec, Henri de Toulouse-Lautrec was born into the world with every material and family advantage and doubtless inherited some of his fanciful imagination from his father, Alphonse, who was a great sportsman, a rider, and loved to wear fancy dress; once his son painted him as old Sachem of *The Last of the Mohicans.* Since young Henri was an aristocrat destined for a leisurely life, his unqualified choice of painting as a vocation was the purest of impulses: a temperamental command by the aesthetic instinct. The liberal type of education he at once began receiving (superintended by a loving mother) had opened the way to a freedom of choice. The margins of his surviving schoolbooks are covered with amazingly lifelike caricatures of comrades, teachers, and parents, as well as of animals. The early painting reproduced in plate 42 shows his humorous gift for setting down his relatives and the animals they rode. His studies of horses turned out to be more extensive and cannier than those of Degas. In Lautrec's equine images, one is confronted by an overwhelming physical feeling for the exact anatomic organism which a horse is – the horse of 1879 (see plate 40) has a finish and comprehension that were prodigious for a 15-year-old artist.

In a work such as that just mentioned, the oil medium is conspicuous not simply as establishing quality of texture, but also (as in Delacroix) as the instrument of drawing: the loaded brush functions also as *linear.* In several years, probably under Degas's influence, Lautrec was to produce finer outlines with his growing attention to portraiture; for example, the image of his mother (plate 47) has a new delicacy of contour. As with Degas, his painting from now on would be a dialectic between precision of drawing and effects of light, especially theatrical effects. Lautrec would portray in many ways the enveloping glare of theatrical light: see *At the Cirque Fernando* (plate 52) and the way he has interpreted in poster terms the "public" light of a music hall or cabaret (plate 59). Degas began with ambitious historical painting but finally gave it up as external to the curious spell which was coming over him as a result of his friendships with musicians and his increasing attendance at the Opera ballet.

Not only was contemporary life calling to painters with the emergent modern spirit; there was a positive disillusionment among them with the pitiless, neutral, impersonal light shed by history – the history so beloved of the academic establishment. Napoleon had been a great popular hero and aroused violent, reverberating political passions. He himself had appealed to the Classical past so that the school of historical painting, blossoming in David, had found a perfect predecessor in Poussin's beautiful reincarnations of ancient statues "in the flesh." Life was a sort of historical frieze composed of pageants in which idealized but specific figures played their parts. The daylight in which Poussin and then David had painted was virtually the universal light of deified Reason, and it seems this same light was being perpetuated in Ingres's polished elaborations of contemporary portraits and purely mythological themes. Delacroix, however, had come along, and with his essentially Republican spirit reanimated the formalism of Classical drawing with an untrammeled energy: his sweeping brush broke the clearly defined volumes of Poussin and David into shadowy, uncertain, threatening masses living in a realm uncontrolled by the uniform daylight of Reason and immune to its calm "dance." Delacroix's female figure of France was the opposite of Napoleon being crowned as a descendant of the Caesars. History was becoming a drama of volatile lights and shadows which the muscularity of Delacroix's brush reflected as a kind of anarchy.

"Classical" daylight had been an *idea* rather than a *reality* and had tended to replace life with traditional myths going into the remote past. Hence it was, precisely speaking, the theater of *history* with which painters of the modern spirit were disillusioned. Life and the history it enclosed was not, after all, an obediently idealistic frieze. The Commune, which broke into the boyhood and youth of the two generations of Impressionists, took place as it were outside the sensibility of the new painting, which had turned away from both history and historical painting in one decisive gesture. The spirit of revolution opposed Reason to tradition but only when it was in the throes of replacing an old political order with a new. None of the true modern artists, after Delacroix and Courbet, felt themselves involved with *political* history-making. When Lautrec showed a French soldier and his horse (plate 40), the last idea in his head was anything patriotic or militaristic. It was animal energy as it merged with human energy, and the dynamic style they achieved together, that he admired. And when, early in his career, Degas painted a Classical theme, Spartan girls challenging boys to wrestle in common nakedness, it was all-important that he was picturing not war but a sport.

Assuredly militarism was not dead, the army still provided ideal careers, and a soldier's uniform (especially combined with a horse) was still a revered spectacle. But the new anti-academic painting turned implacably to nature and painted the "holiday" picture whose peculiar note had been sounded by Manet's *Le Déjeuner sur l'herbe* and would be made heroic by Seurat's *La Grande Jatte.* The keynote was observation of humanity when at peace with itself amid peaceful natural surroundings: gardens and parks as well as hillsides. Just the same, the senior Degas and the junior Lautrec did not become landscape painters, nor did they, like certain Impressionists, paint nature as a sort of Eden peopled by nudes. Our two painters became, above all the rest, significantly *urban.* Their portraits were usually done with the subjects at home or in the painter's studio; or, if theatrical people, at dance or music halls, on stage at the Opera, or in the circus. Exceptions occurred in Lautrec's case when he portrayed a subject in some garden spot.

Eventually both Degas and Lautrec suffered physical injuries that were to give them lifetime infirmities; with the latter and very soon, it was a fatal deformity. Degas, serving during the Commune in the National Guard, caught a severe chill and emerged with his eyesight impaired: an affliction mild at first but growing worse with age. When Lautrec was about fourteen, he broke first one leg and then the other through bad falls. His sufferings were terrible, and after a lengthy convalescence he found himself deformed by weak, short legs that refused to keep up with

Degas *Studies of Horses*

the rest of his growth. He was to remain stunted all his life. Yet neither the young count's courage nor his zeal for painting was lessened by this trial of body and spirit; in fact, through it all, he not only painted but maintained a very extraordinary good humor. For the remainder of his life he was to assume, by and large, that he was normal and could be as active as anyone else; at the same time, he was witty at his own expense on occasions when his incapacity was involved. Like his father, he developed a stylish, personal manner, even special habits of speech and vocabulary, as if he were playing some part on the stage.

Both artists plunged themselves into the days and nights of Parisian life in order to see it as it looked and moved – to discover a new truth in living appearances; in other words, these two, beyond all artists of their time, rebelled against the Classical dreams of the Academicians by seeking to show, as if holding up a mirror, the self-conscious ways in which society behaved: as its various levels and spheres characteristically, consciously conceived themselves. The present, not the past, was the "history" they started in earnest to paint. It wasn't that they did on-the-spot sketches parallel with the truths of photography. Of course, more or less, portraits were done in this way during the initial stages. But the method followed by Degas and Lautrec, to obtain their brilliant truthfulness as painters of "the real," must be called visual saturation.

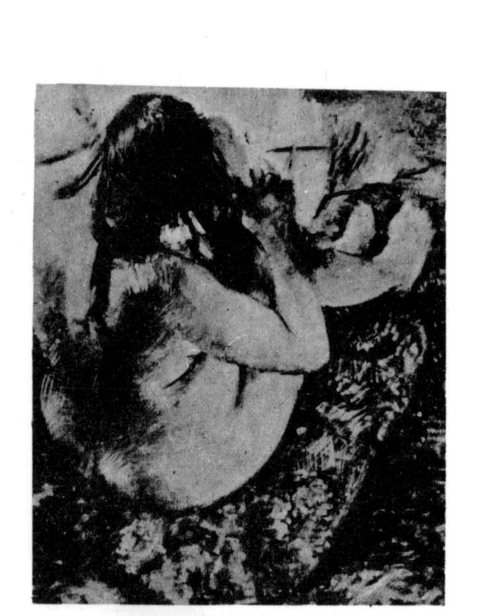

Degas *A Woman Doing Her Coiffure*
about 1881

Mutually, their attitude toward their craft was intensely studious and duly humble. Degas in particular, having started with more heroic ambitions than Lautrec, felt the difficulty ahead of him in suiting his conversion of tradition to the living image of Paris after which he yearned. In a notebook kept in his youth, he had written: "Oh, Giotto, don't prevent me from seeing Paris; and you, Paris, don't prevent me from seeing Giotto." His thoughtful and prayerful invocation, remarkably enough, was rewarded. By constantly going to rehearsals and dancing classes, Degas learned not only the dance poses themselves but also the dancers' habits of movement, the transitions from one pose to another; thus, although he would make a few sketches on the spot, his true evocation of dancers and dance groups came when he was by himself in his studio and suddenly a very precise moment emerged from the flickers of memory, a certain relationship of dancers ready to dance or in the flux of dancing, and this he would proceed to reconstruct, attitude by attitude, fragment by fragment; such a "moment," involving a stageful of dancers, may be found in plate 19.

Yet a true study of Degas's scenes, particularly those of rehearsals and dancing classes, reveals that, despite the glamor and glitter which he gave ballerinas in action on stage (plates 24, 25, and 26), he was really more absorbed by the harsh discipline which comprised a dancer's training: the artifice of attitude and choreographic figure into which dancers must learn to force their limbs. He would show the butterfly spreading her wings, yet some almost morbid fascination compelled him also to show the fledgling dancer struggling out of her cocoon in all the eager awkwardness of her immaturity. This obsessed interest of the artist came to be reflected, in later years, by his many nude women caught at moments of their toilet when they were oddly contorted or doubled over (see plates 30 and 34).

Lautrec, for his part, was drawn to the more popular dance stage and dances of the ballroom, such as the quadrille, especially because of the bizarre personalities of some of the stars. Such dancing was not the realm of the airily pointed toe but, on the contrary, of wild kicks which seemed typically to "lead" with the heel rather than the toe. Consult plate 60, and the comment on it, for an image of this sort of dancing. Out of these vulgar dances – at times with their own interest and even finesse – Lautrec was to develop his caricatural style of portrayal so close to life as it was. He was inspired by all the strangeness of genius, such as that of the fantastic-looking singer and *diseuse* Yvette Guilbert.

Degas *Self-Portrait,* 1854-55

Unlike Lautrec, Degas was not so much interested in individual performers as in the type-dancer transformed by light and gauze and arabesque into a creature of generic illusion: part woman, part dream. He never quite lost sight of the real woman in his dancers, but he revealed her as an organism which had devoted her womanhood to a complete transformation, artificializing while sublimating herself. Almost entirely abandoning oil paint after 1880, Degas employed the pastel texture to suggest such artifice as tangible: pastel in several layers, both smooth and grainy, expressed the surfaces of powdered faces, stockinged legs, and satin shoes, even the ambivalent resistance of stiff but crushable gauze.

However much that Degas made use of his privilege of going anywhere in the theater – backstage and to rehearsal rooms – he was always the gentleman spectator, the devotee in a stage box; never, in any clear sense, the star's lover or her dressing-room suitor. We find in Lautrec's work, on the other hand, an intimacy with dressing rooms (plates 68, 72 and 74) and the easy fraternity of the cabaret or dance hall, where he could chat

a way valid, did not mean the flattery of rendering anything grand or romantic; it meant no attempt to depict these women as anything but what, in the most literal sense, they were. Lautrec wished to paint as accurately as possible their humanity, and in this very accuracy (wholly without satire or moral prejudice) to show his essential respect and, paradoxically, his brotherly fondness.

The private flesh and its pursuits are always, in an artist's case, a matter apart from his art. So it was with the luxurious bachelor Lautrec and the aesthetic bachelor Degas, neither of whom was bothered by lack of money. Lautrec drank a great deal, liked orgiastic parties, and was always in brothels – the legendary life that led to his breakdown. Degas led the life of a gentleman aesthete while outside his studio. True, he also did some brothel scenes, but they lack the deep, knowing sense of familiarity exuded by Lautrec's more numerous images of this kind. It must be remembered that both these artists had posed themselves a heroic lifetime project: that of scrutinizing Paris itself and of compassing the whole gamut of what might be called Parisian womanhood. Degas's whores, like his laundresses, are simply another essential set of female models, both being, however, subordinate to his dancers. Not to be outdone, Lautrec also painted laundresses and shopgirls. Much is told us about Degas's attitude toward love by two sentences from a letter written to a friend in 1886: "I am growing old in all but my heart, and even that has a faded air. The ballet dancers have stitched it up in a pink satin bag, dusty, rose-colored satin, like their dancing shoes."

Lautrec

The realism of Degas and Lautrec alike, concentrating on aesthetic and emotional aspects of life with which they were in the closest touch, is bound to carry with it what psychology has called fetichism. Despite his objectivity, and his human sympathy, Lautrec undoubtedly found in the milieu of brothels something both soothing and seductive to his senses: the availability of the flesh – easy, natural, without moral or social ties. Moreover, the exciting clamor and ceaseless stir of dance halls, the intoxication of music as well as drink, provided ceaseless stimulation and created a deep need in Lautrec, like the need for a drug. His images of circus grotesquerie, superlatively true and comic, necessarily produced a sort of empathy in an artist who caricatured himself, being deformed, as one also set apart from normalcy. It is almost meaningless to say that such a man "fell in love"; it is much more plausible to say that he nourished

← **Degas** *Artist and Model*

Montage photo *Lautrec Painting Lautrec*, about 1890

passionate fantasies, perhaps a more or less hidden fetichism for objects of desire beyond his reach, while his carnal indulgences formed a rather mechanical addiction. Of course, it is always possible to take the view of romantic fiction and speculate on inadequate evidence.

Degas's relations with women – to take an equally plausible approach – must be read through his devotion to the ballerina's theatrical image (to which he even wrote poems), since what we know of these things indicates that he loved essentially through the heart rather than with the senses themselves. His array of dance pictures is like an inquisition into the ordeal of an initiation rite in which girls suffer both pain and exhaustion in order to reach their supernatural moments of glory on stage: an apotheosis. The study of the endless suite of Degas's dancers shows beyond doubt that his eye was as much alive to the ugliness and strained effort of a ballerina's training as to those moments of grace when she was transformed on stage into a princess or a fairy. He perceived the same unpretty angularity and contortion in the nude women engaged in making their toilets. Thus it was logical that, during the eighties, he began doing sculptural sketches of dancers going through their exercises and, because nearly always nudes, altogether stripped of theatrical illusion. However clever and spontaneous as plastic works, they seem hard, strange, in the monochrome darkness of their bronze hue. The effect of these very small figures (see plates 37 and 39) has nothing of the voluptuous aestheticism of Degas's pastel images; indeed, they seem cruelly exiled from the refined sensuousness of the pastels, where color and light make dancers into poetic apparitions.

At first introducing a well-defined hatch into his pastel work, Degas eventually made this medium more and more complicated with superimposed and sometimes wetted layers, so that the final surface was somewhat like the powdered and repowdered cheek of a perspiring ballerina; the "crusty" texture seen in plate 36 – while it may have been inspired by the presence of moist heat since it is a bathroom scene – appears in the later dance scenes like the light-drenched texture of a gauze tutu: something insistently tactile in look. The pronounced fuzziness of texture and the heavier, vaguer outlines of Degas's later pastel technique (see plate 33), which had less detail, is attributed by some to his failing eyesight, but surely it is also due to the ultra-crystallization of a whole life's sensuousness: an accruant climax of touching transposed to seeing. Degas had the idea of delving, penetrating – "appearance" was in a way an illusion concealing the hard rudiments of the lurking truth. Ordinary observers get too much accustomed to theatrical illusion, to the dazzlement of its lights; to Degas, such "dazzlement" posed analytical problems which he dedicated himself at length to solving. He even hated to consider a picture quite finished, and time and again would apply wistfully to some owner to have it back so as to add a few all-important touches.

Yvette Guilbert

While regarded in general as an Impressionist, and admitted by the group to their official company, Degas, even as Lautrec, remained a special case, and perhaps more than other new painters of his generation, he increasingly sought solitude as the years passed. For Lautrec, both the time of living and the time of art would be rather stingy. As obviously accomplished as he was, he was not easily classified, and when his first show took place in 1893, even Degas passed a somewhat cursory, if genially ironic, judgment on him. "My dear Lautrec," he addressed him, after passing through hurriedly, "it's quite evident that you belong to the establishment." Some had the impression, doubtless owing to his posters and the surface frivolity of many of his subjects, that he was no more than a "fashionable amateur." In fact, though it was asserted that he had tried to succeed with "ugliness" rather than "charm," a good portion of the art world took a favorable view of his work.

All "climaxes" in Degas's life were privately handled and unhurried. In Lautrec's life, perforce, both profession and private personality were involved in fatal wreckage when, in 1899, at the peak of his technical powers, he suffered a collapse from debauchery and drink and had to retire to a mental sanitarium for a long cure. Veritably he had lived the social life of prostitutes, staying in a borthel for days, and even receiving his friends there. If his images of life in brothel are nearly all now at the Toulouse-Lautrec Museum in Albi, it is because he discreetly did not exhibit or try to sell these pictures, showing them only to a few close friends. Degas's dancers gradually won, inevitably, a unique and magnetic niche for themselves if only because they glorified a thoroughly French institution (the Opera ballet) in a thoroughly French manner.

When Lautrec recovered and was back in circulation and at his easel, columns of print declared that he had been doomed by his doctors; previously, during his illness, he had been spoken of as dead or hopelessly insane. Journalism, as usual, gave expression to the most violent and

Lautrec *Divan Japonais,* 1892

scandalous rumors; it was said outright that a man so monstrously crippled and wantonly self-indulgent was bound to go mad, and to this was added, when his death was announced in 1901, the cruel opinion that he had been fated to destroy himself. In answer, a few loyal voices were raised in his defense, one writer (in the interim when he was still alive) having optimistically claimed that Lautrec had "never felt better in his life."

Though he did not, like van Gogh, take his own life, Lautrec's experience with insanity parallels van Gogh's, because he too died a couple of years after his internment. If we examine Lautrec's technique in certain works (take the portrait of Madame Gortzikoff, plate 63), we find a nervously apparent stroking that may have been fortified by the example of van Gogh's manner: in Paris the two had had a fleeting but mutually interested contact. Degas, living until 1917, faded, as it were, from his long and dedicated life as an artist; Lautrec went very prematurely in the grim backwash of his psychological disaster. Each man left a unique and precious heritage: masterly works that are both social documents (part of *history,* after all!) and among the most refined achievements of plastic sensibility in the art which bridged the nineteenth and twentieth centuries.

Description of the color plates

1. *Self-portrait*
1862
Oil
92.1 x 68.9cm
National Gallery of Art, Washington D. C.

In this self-view of the dandy, thinker, and member of the *beau monde,* much is told and predicted of Degas the man and painter. The drawing is virtually classic in accuracy and firmness, yet outlines and textures have that quality of illusionism which the Impressionists were about to isolate as a truth of aesthetic perception. Note the transparently painted left sleeve, helping to bring forward the landscape painting behind it, and the rough treatment of the left hand in comparison with the right, as if the eye had not focused the same way on each; also note how the canvas weave shows in Degas's face as well as in the painting within the painting.

2/3. *The Belleli Family*
1860-62
Oil
200.0 x 250.0cm
The Louvre, Paris

Family portraits were of course high-bourgeois conventions. Here Degas, with his first such attempt, has made an artful composition on a scale ambitiously heroic for this genre. He would be a tireless seeker of stable forms no matter how impressionistically painted. Of course the two girls' large white aprons balance one another admirably, while their mother's pyramidal shape emphasizes the decorative effect. Just as one girl's clasp of hands over her stomach varies the pattern, the symmetry of her sister is daringly modified by having her leg invisible beneath her – this irregularity of balanced form (probably Japanese in origin) would be one of the great problems Degas set himself. He was already in pursuit of the lifelikeness that was "casual."

4. *Portrait of a Woman*
1861
Oil
41.0 x 29.0cm
Musée des Beaux-Arts, Algeria

Surely a good portrait, this, yet rather phantasmal for Degas's period. The hands, the dress below the waist, are all sketchy, painted virtually in terms of highlights, while what looks like a leafy trellis behind the woman is portrayed with obvious paint strokes. At the same time, the volumes of the body and face are as clearly defined as in any Renaissance work. The mauve-gray-blue tonality is thoroughly Parisian.

5. *Self-portrait*
1854-55
Oil
81.0 x 64.5cm
The Louvre, Paris

Preceding in date the self-portrait of plate 1, this Degas is younger and moodier but just as much, as to painting, a budding Impressionist. In arrangement recalling fine Renaissance portraits of men, it already allows clarity of drawing to fall away into shadow and to "neglect" the hands. The beautifully painted head hangs in space as a sort of mirage, while the pouting lips reinforce the dreamy depth of the eyes.

Degas *Study of Violin Player* →
Degas *Hair* (Page 108)

Degas

6. *Gentlemen's Race: Before the Start*
1862
Oil
48.5 x 61.0cm
The Louvre, Paris

Artist and man of the world were to blend exquisitely in Degas. The sport of horse racing was as fashionable in the elegant world as the art of the dance, which was to obsess this painter even more. He has vividly picked out, in what looks like an overcast afternoon, the glowing colors of the jockeys' outfits, to which he has subordinated the darker values of their mounts, in turn suppressing into vague tokens the distant crowd and the horizon. This technique, with its diminishing edges, serves to suggest the modern concern of arresting time in its passage.

7. *Start of the Chase*
1864–68
Oil
70.0 x 89.0cm
Private Collection, Paris

Fox hunting, too, was a gentleman's sport not to be overlooked. Here Degas has played with the dawn-touched shapes of red-and-white horsemen who seem to be coming into existence with the day. Note how the further legs of the horse at near left have been painted only in outline as if, supernaturally, the sunlight were showing through them. Perhaps a trace of morning mist makes them look that way. The illusionism, of course, disturbed the academicians: it was too "natural."

8. *Portrait of a Young Woman*
1867
Oil
27.0 x 22.0cm
The Louvre, Paris

The thin layer of paint portraying this charming head assists the effect of general transparency as much as does the reliance on illuminated surface to shape the lady's features. The fineness of the drawing remains subsidiary. Whistler would exaggerate these same effects into his liquescent impressionism. The passage of warm light on the ear and cheekbone is especially characteristic, as are the glints of light in the bandeau.

9. *Mademoiselle Dobigny*
1869
Oil
31.0 x 26.0cm
Private Collection, Zurich

The very pretty young lady (of the rounded popular type) has all the look of being the subject of a commissioned portrait – at least, Degas has reverted for some reason to a much more academic manner than he had developed by this time. However debonair the treatment of the dress, the lady's features have been clearly drawn as solid flesh seen in unambiguous light and shade.

10. *Musicians of the Orchestra*
1868–69
Oil
56.5 x 46.0cm
The Louvre, Paris

A lover of music and the theater, Degas had the customary privilege of accredited individuals to go back stage and everywhere in the theater. The scene here is the Opera House, whose musicians he knew as friends and whose dancers he was quickly getting to know. Each face here, unquestionably, is a portrait. The medley of clear masculine visages makes an arresting contrast with the

Degas *After the Bath* (Page 109)
← **Degas** *Sketch of Dancer with Tambourine*

floating luminous shapes of the dancers on stage. The general layout of the scene is, of course, unconventional.

11. *The Violoncellist Pillet*
1868–69
Oil
50.5 x 61.0cm
The Louvre, Paris

Here is an honorific portrait of a friend of Degas's in which, slyly, he has inserted a delicate note of pomposity by including the "official" portrait of an orchestra hanging on the wall. The grouped instruments impart a somewhat surprising emphasis to the right side of the picture, even though they are present to balance the human figure on the left.

12. *Portrait of Monsieur Ruelle*
1862
Oil
44.0 x 36.0cm
Musée des Beaux-Arts, Lyon

Another tribute to a musician, this is a stately work in which Degas has conscientiously caught, it would seem, a very true physiognomic likeness while adhering to his peculiar impressionistic style. The flesh tone is admirably set off by the greenish background, while the relation between the prominent hand and the face, again, is reminiscent of Renaissance portraits.

13. *Race Horses: Before the Grandstand*
1869–72
Pastel
46.0 x 61.0cm
The Louvre, Paris

In a work of Post-Impressionistic atmosphere, this manner of Degas will influence Lautrec's poster style. The grandstand and its occupants are portrayed in flat washes and a few essential lines. The light drenches everything. Note the curious way in which the jockey, centaur-like, replaces the horse's unseen neck and head. The moving horse disappearing past the margin is characteristically Degas: the *modern* way of arresting time in its flight.

14. *Madame Camus at the Piano*
1869–72
Oil
139.0 x 94.0cm
Private Collection, Zurich

Female musicians would also, naturally, engage Degas's interest. This lady, posing by music sheets whose black marks are very conspicuous, has the air of consciously accepting a compliment. There are clever elements in the work, but among Degas's many brilliant portraits it is a not-so-happy one. It was not completed till three years had passed. The Commune had taken place meantime, and while Degas served in the artillery of the National Guard, he had caught a chill and found his eyesight impaired. His eyes were to trouble him throughout his life.

15. *Mademoiselle Dihau at the Piano*
1869–72
Oil
45.0 x 32.0cm
The Louvre, Paris

The face of this female musician, with its eloquent and subtle expression of personality, is finely poised in juncture with the wavy diagonal made by the arm and placed in pointed contrast with the open music score. The visible portion of the hand at bottom left and the two luminous spots (one behind the pianist's bonnet) lead the eye skilfully along the diagonal made by the dense shade in the work's lower right. The flamelike touch on the bonnet has a similar function in relation to the red of lips and cheek.

16. *The Pedicure*
1873
Oil
61.0 x 46.0cm
The Louvre, Paris

Once more Degas exploits transparent pale colors to suggest distance, here in a superb interior and a subject that barely hints of a refined morbidity. The very fact that the little girl is swathed in a towel or sheet suggests her nakedness. The tub and the draped chair will become very familiar motifs of Degas's subjects. The partial intervention of the drape between us and the operation being performed by the doctor causes the picture to stir with the faint breath of insinuation.

17. *The Man and the Puppet*
1873
Oil
41.0 x 27.0cm
National Gallery of Art,
Washington D. C.

It is hardly necessary to be told that the man is the artist himself. Degas had begun being one of the theater's most loyal habitués. He has devised a brilliant parable of his art in which the life-sized female puppet betrays the illusionism of painting. She must have made more than one of his sitters a trifle uncomfortable. The sketchy figures in the visible paintings are only one or two removes from the artificiality of the puppet – posed as she is, awry. One may interpret the painter's gaze as Mephistophelian: actual human figures in his work will echo the puppet's distorted attitude. By this route, Degas deemed himself discoverer of a new truth in painting: the artifice of life itself.

18. *The Dancing Class*
1874
Oil
85.0 x 75.0cm
The Louvre, Paris

Degas's preeminent theme makes one of its crucial appearances: he will be tireless in painting dancing girls. Strikingly, the colors of their ribbons recall the costumes of jockeys. The intimation of a dancer's training as something rigid and a little cruel is conveyed not only by the assertive stance of the dancing master but also by the rather massive stick he plants on the floor before him. The filmy flare of a ballerina's skirt will become for this artist a supreme sign of sensibility – as if it were a star or a princely crest.

19. *Ballet Rehearsal on Stage*
1874
Oil
66.0 x 82.0cm
The Louvre, Paris

The rosy *grisaille* of this work's monotone coloration is a phase of the theater's transformation, as if all local colors were driven away by the uniform saturation of the footlights. The ingenious grouping of the dancers crystallizes Degas's *penchant* for a subject in which he will have no rivals. He had discovered just how to suggest the rest and restlessness of dancers about to begin rehearsal:

the sudden yet natural passing of stillness into movement and movement into stillness.

20/21. *At the Races: Amateur Jockeys before the Grandstand*
1877–80
Oil
66.0 x 81.0cm
The Louvre, Paris

Degas has caught beautifully the rich, informal commotion of moments experienced by gentlemen who ride "for fun." The lady in the carriage is probably admiring her husband or her lover, her son or her brother, as a jockey. Figures entering or leaving the visible scene, and partly cut off by the margin, will be a trait of Degas – a characteristic modern way of showing the ceaseless flow of life. Compare the horse dashing in here with the one dashing out in plate 13. The detail shows the meticulous roughness of Degas's drawing. Several years before starting this work, he had officially joined the Impressionist group for its first exhibition.

22/23. *At the Ambassadeurs: Café Concert*
1876–77
Pastel
37.0 x 27.0cm
Musée des Beaux-Arts, Lyon

Theatrical subjects among all others are susceptible of presenting moments passing and illusionistic. For Degas, this was an ideal of truth telling. Here he shows how closely he has observed the busy scene of a concert performance to put its atmosphere (especially its play of light) into, as it were, a nutshell. Everything is more or less in movement: heads in the audience turning, the ladies on the platform gesturing or stirring, even the musical instruments vibrating. The work is prophetically "cinematic." The detail emphasizes how this has been achieved plastically. The lines of profiles tend to break and fuse with encroaching light and color; the hand of the cornet player, presumably in motion, is barely suggested. And notice the singer's extended arm: the hand is quite blurred, as if in motion; this is a tiny intimation of the next century's Futurism.

24. *Dancer Bowing: End of an Arabesque*
1877
Pastel
67.4 x 38.0cm
The Louvre, Paris

Enthralled by his constant proximity with dancers, Degas now does images of them as if they were seen from a stage box or in the filmic close-up still to be invented. Pastel, with its fragile touch, seemed the ideal medium for the swift flicker of illuminated dancers whose white tutus absorbed the light at its brightest and seemed to emit flashes. The dancers' group in the background is beautifully articulated with light and color. Degas sought always the effects of light on things, never light itself. Oil paint he considered unfit to express the flitting and englamored light shed by dancers.

25. *The Star; or Dancer on Stage*
1878
Pastel
60.0 x 44.0cm
The Louvre, Paris

The dancer is in motion and her skirt is as much like an opalescent patch of light as like gauze. In strict perspective, as seen from above, her body seems distorted and yet her attitude is perfectly free and natural. The development of artificial postures of the body, a cultivated thing in dancers, never ceased to fascinate Degas. Note how abstractly sketched is all the background material – and how convincing it is for that very reason. The artist was aware that dancers and their costumes brought flower colors into intense artificial light.

26. *Dancer with Bouquet, Bowing*
1877
Pastel
75.0 x 78.0cm
The Louvre, Paris

A theatrical moment beautifully imagined and infallibly caught. The constantly observant Degas, making only hasty sketches in the theater and classroom, derived all his final conceptions of dancers from memory while in his studio. One senses the gauze itself, the powder, the silk on this pink and yellow ballerina with her breathlessly open mouth. She is still in motion, the bent knee not quite at the climax of the bow. The dry pastel lies on top of the pasty surface to express texture and highlight. By now, there was a distinct thing that could be called a "Degas surface."

27. *The Ironers*
1884
Pastel
76.0 x 81.5cm
The Louvre, Paris

For these two laundresses – one at work, the other so obviously taking time out for a nip – Degas uses heavier pressure with his medium and thicker outlines: they are not such airy creatures as ballerinas. The picture caused some sneering criticism; the story about it was that the artist had based the yawning laundress on a character from one of Zola's novels. Though there are virtually no prismatic effects here, the local colors and their warm and cool gamut have a way of melting suggestively into each other so that the work's total look is opalescent.

28. *Injured Jockey and Bolting Horse*
1866
Oil
180.0 x 151.0cm
Private Collection, Paris

An earlier work, and far from academic, this rendering of a common accident has a strange, gratuitous, whimsical air. The jockey's prostrate figure is remarkably flat in dimension, somewhat puppet-like (see plate 17), and the horse (painted before photographic experiments revealed the true action of a running horse) rather wooden in its "rocking horse" posture. The artist's vein of morbidity peeps out, stirring up one's wonder. The fluffy white clouds in the light-blue sky contrast with the somber tone of the hillside, as if it were under shadow.

29. *Portrait of Zacharie Zacharian*
1885
Pastel
39.0 x 39.0cm
Private Collection, Paris

Degas was a collector of images of the smart world of Paris. This portrait of a great gentleman, his worldly gaze and rather arrogant mouth very well caught behind the carefully tended beard, is full of the hatching technique of the artist's later manner. The hatch is carried out in the flesh tones of the face, but more delicately than elsewhere, and fuses ideally with the hairs of the beard. Notice the subtlety of the cool highlights on the fingers, where the stretched skin is less rosy.

30. *After the Bath: Woman Wiping Her Feet*
1886
Pastel
54.3 x 52.4cm
The Louvre, Paris

The increasing graininess of Degas's pastel surface in his later period conveys more sensuousness, which is especially in keeping with his domestic nudes, always women in various stages of their toilet. The posture here makes a curious design yet looks eminently natural. The short vertical marks breaking the body's smooth sweep of contour are Degas's method of uniting objects with their surroundings and making a single plane of the atmosphere. The hatching, of course, suggests at once density and transparence.

31. *After the Bath: Woman Wiping Her Neck*
1898
Pastel
62.2 x 65.0cm
The Louvre, Paris

So fertile of domestic nudes, Degas (now aged 64) had reached, as here, a broader and broader assurance. There is a charming spontaneity about this one: the moment of action is as finely calculated as the bow of a ballerina. The shaded and lighted surface of the skin is wonderfully natural and controlled by the bold hatching. There is, too, a new freedom in the treatment of the background. Taken unawares, one is struck by the impression that the decoratively patterned panel seen just above the woman is very close to the complex mottling of the American abstract painter Jackson Pollock.

32. *Green Dancers*
1899
Pastel
Private Collection, Paris

Here there is no distinction between local color and the light which apparently bathes the dancers. The now fluid outlines and the open hatching combine to express momentariness and hurry, as if the curtain were about to go up or at least as if the dancers were on the point of making an entrance. There is a curious confusion about the two central dancers – is the nearer one adjusting only her own costume or also that of the dancer beyond her? The third dancer, if already poised to go on stage, must be annoyed with her lagging mates, who thus would be not quite ready.

33. *Two Dancers*
1897
Pastel

The indefatigable Degas, pursuing the refinements of craft as assiduously as his lifetime motifs, has produced one of his stunning triumphs here. It is not just that the poses are absolutely authentic but that, together with this fact, he has used his medium (mostly a coarse kind of frosting) to present light-drenched textures at their maximum effect of optical truth and lyricism of feeling. The two dancers are veritable creatures of light and color as if they truly existed only in these costumes, lighted by this light, so that when off the stage and seen as just women, they would be unrecognizable: denizens of a quite different world. One feels, in a really uncanny sense, that they are as much butterflies as human beings. The dark underpainting, showing uneven outlines and guaranteeing their solidity, seems shadow rather than substance.

34. *Woman at Her Toilet*
1905–07
Pastel
77.0 x 70.0cm
Private Collection, Paris

Having long set himself the portrayal of the action postures of nude women at their toilets, Degas has grown to be a past master of nature's automatic contortions of the body. One is struck by the openness and variety of the hatching technique here, lending so much spontaneity to the routine gesture. The shading on the body, seeming at a glance all black, is actually mixed with some blue. It is remarkable how well the distinct strokes of rose over the paper's tone blend into natural flesh color. The painter has learned his anatomic drawing by heart. Yet the woman's black outlines are not "naturalistically" smooth and round but are done with subtle angles.

35. *Madame Rouart and Her Children*
1905
Pastel
160.0 x 141.0cm
Musée du Petit-Palais, Paris

High mastery increases an artist's daring and brings to light his inveterate obsessions. Degas possessed a virtually cinematic interest in portraying a stage of progressive action, implying as clearly the instants that went before as those that were to come. It is as if the mother here had determined to rise against her child's will and the child had sought to detain her with a hand. Their facial expressions confirm this. On the other hand, making a movement in a direction opposite to her mother's, the older child seems just to have turned and leaned – perhaps in a huff, perhaps idly – against the back of the chair in which she sits. The treatment of the whole surface is rather flat except for the bust of the mother, which thus has the look of projecting from the picture plane like a bas-relief. The calligraphic scrawl in the background is of distinct technical interest.

36. *Woman in the Bath*
1892
Pastel
Art Gallery of Toronto, Canada

The very grainy texture of a work abandoning the hatching technique is extremely sensuous and saturated with the bright hues which characterized Bonnard's treatment of the same subject. It is as if the atmosphere were full of steam since the heavy pastel medium, though worked openly, has been made fluid to suggest the element of water. Note how the outlines are blurred in keeping with this general feeling. The hot reflections on the woman's side are an enigmatic orange, which in effect would symbolize the heat of the water presumably lying in the tub. The work is full of charm and eloquence: a masterpiece of Impressionist form and color.

37. *Dancer*
1882
Bronze
The Louvre, Paris

During a certain period, Degas also essayed putting his dancers into sculptured form. A great range of figures, all on a small scale, exist. They are nude with very few exceptions: one is a very young dancer dressed in an actual gauze tutu. As with his painted figures, the artist's preoccupation is with the posture rather than with the flesh and its sensuality (which so absorbed a painter such as Renoir). The wonderfully delicate skin surfaces and spontaneous action of Degas's pastels tend to vanish in his sculptural sketches and be replaced with gymnastic poses of the dancer's technical training; logically, the theatrical personality also tends to disappear.

38. *Horse*
Bronze
The Louvre, Paris

Degas's other typical object of interest, horses, also took on the sculptural medium, and likewise became expressions of a body in motion. This artist's statues utterly contradicted, both plastically and as to scale, sculpture's traditional identity as restfully monumental mass. To some extent, Rodin had succeeded in modifying this tradition by introducing into sculpture a sense of nervous surface and progressive movement. Degas, as this rearing horse impressively conveys, debonairly ignored all "sculptural repose."

39. *Dancer*
1882–92
Bronze
50.5cm
Bridgestone Gallery, Tokyo

The primary absorption of the artist with pose rather than anatomy is underlined by this dancer's extremely rough surface. As successful as the attitude is, as anatomically adept, one must abandon one's taste for the free ease and poetic ingratiation of Degas's painted dancers so as to appreciate, here, the charm of naked limbs dedicated to the training of the body by difficult exertion. Conceiving this dedication in utter nudity, Degas in a way purifies while impersonalizing his old obsession with "dislocative" gesture.

Lautrec *Head of La Goulue* →
Lautrec *At the Moulin Rouge: La Goulue and La Mome Fromage* (Page 120)

40. *Artilleryman Saddling His Horse*
1879
Oil
50.5 x 37.5cm
Musée Toulouse-Lautrec, Albi

Toulouse-Lautrec, only fifteen when he painted this, grew up in an art world toned through and through with Impressionism, whose manners he proceeded to adapt with brilliant ease. There is a curt, angular snap to the strokes here, applied with a vigor as broad as Delacroix's. The glistening gray surface of the splendid horse seems to vibrate with all its inner dynamic life while its busy master has a similarly appealing energy and ranginess. Playfully, aptly, Lautrec makes the atmosphere and the ground itself "dance" with liveliness.

41. *Céleyran: View of a Vineyard*
1880
Oil
16.5 x 23.9cm
Musée Toulouse-Lautrec, Albi

Céleyran was the name of the artist's family estate and of course its chateau. Confining himself almost wholly to greens and browns, with only slight suggestion of a heated blue sky, Lautrec has skilfully executed a landscape which has no outstanding features. In its simplicity and strength of suggestiveness, it is a tour-de-force. The bold stroking betrays a loaded brush, already a perfect instrument of impressionistic texture.

42. *Raoul Tapié of Céleyran*
1881
Oil
60.0 x 50.0cm
Private Collection, Paris

The artist's interest in humor and character verging on caricature is foretold by the glimpse of his young cousin on a balking donkey. The paint is very energetic without attempting the twinkling iridescence of other Impressionists; the animal's brown coat is straightforward despite the cool glints it borrows from the open air. The dotting in the landscape, to give variety of color tone, is unsystematic and imparts to the whole a charming spontaneity.

43. *Nude Study: Woman Seated on a Divan*
1882
Oil
55.0 x 46.0cm
Musée Toulouse-Lautrec, Albi

As much a devoted observer of the unclothed female as Degas, Lautrec concentrated more on particular personality and restfully expressive pose. He has grasped here a wonderful sense of a daylit interior: one might almost guess the hour, since the angle of light falling on the face and bust seems near the meridian. The woman seems the perfect model of the Paris studio of this period. One might suppose that the blue and rose arrangement of her environment will eventually attract Picasso's attention.

44. *A Laborer at Céleyran*
1882
Oil
60.0 x 42.0cm
Musée Toulouse-Lautrec, Albi

One can imagine the diminutive artist, busy on location around the chateau, requesting (and perhaps paying) this man to spend some of his leisure time posing for a portrait. Lautrec sought in his sitters not so much the unique person – that mystic essence of human identity – as his outer characteristics, what he usually showed the world. But to this is always given, no matter how

Lautrec *Marcelle* (Page 121)
← **Lautrec** *Napoleon I on Horseback*

casual-seeming the work, the most careful attention. The man's expression, while distant from the point of view, seems exactly portrayed. The intruding foliage, the swirling grass, add elements of interest.

45. *Still Life*
1882
Oil
27.0 x 22.0cm
Musée Toulouse-Lautrec, Albi

The artist must have been studying and perhaps brooding on the works of painters such as Monet and Renoir when he did this work. He is still shy of strong prisms, however, and mingles with restraint the warm and cool reflections in glass and decanter, boat and water. It is a painting whose authorship, standing open, might be hard to decide. Comparing the arrangement of strokes in the foreground with those seen in the previous plate would assist in the attribution.

46. *Old Woman Seated on a Bench at Céleyran*
1882
Oil
53.0 x 44.0cm
Musée Toulouse-Lautrec, Albi

A blue-green spectrum, cleverly warmed up throughout, places this old woman securely in pale daylight. Her slightly averted profile, perhaps expressing a peasantlike shyness, is adroitly limned by Lautrec's conscientious drawing, always loyal to facial character. The slump of age and a lifetime of labor are in the heavy, resting body, complementing the wistful gleam of spirit which just as clearly emanates from her oblique, undirected gaze.

47. *La Comtesse A. de Toulouse-Lautrec*
1883
Oil
93.5 x 81.0cm
Musée Toulouse-Lautrec, Albi

A respectful tenderness achieved by superb drawing and meticulous painting stamps this image of the artist's mother. The effect of figure and background is quiet, even sedate, a fact that becomes very remarkable when one registers the liveliness of the strokes which, especially in the Countess's surroundings, go in so many different directions. Lautrec demonstrates he is already a master of his craft. The slightly sad facial expression, emphasized by the lowered eyelids, the large sensitive hands, full of dignity yet a bit nervous, have no hint of the sentimentality which would have spoiled the work's perfect conception.

48/49. *The Ball at the Moulin de la Galette*
1889
Oil
90.0 x 100.0cm
Art Institute of Chicago

Joining Degas as a connoisseur of Parisian life, Lautrec here essays a subject already treated by Renoir in one of his famous pictures. Although a nobleman, Lautrec has left us much the racier version, seeking out the most typical qualities of a place where the working classes came to enjoy and disport themselves. The wide-open hatching which marks the dancers in the background, together with individualizing details, seems to catch the true spice of this Parisian phenomenon. The nearest woman, with her pretty, made-up face, is quite ready to flirt while the pair a little removed from her wait stolidly for their opportunities. The seated male spectator is patently rather stiff in his requirements for a partner (or is he longing to pounce on someone already engaged?). Lautrec's color here is richer, at once more local and keyed up in shadowy iridescence.

50. *The Day of First Communion*
1888
Oil
65.0 x 37.0cm
Musée des Augustins, Toulouse

The artist's developing caricatural bent makes an appearance in a straight satire on the middle class. The coarse brown board on which he will do many works also becomes evident. It is a picture where the details matter more than anything else – they can be picked out, with appropriate chuckles, one by one. In fact, is not overwhelming detail exactly what has absorbed this family in preparing for the serious event to which they are now on their way?

51. *At the Races*
1899
Oil
45.0 x 53.0cm
Musée Toulouse-Lautrec, Albi

Though at a later time than Degas, Lautrec was also much attracted to the elegant sporting world of horses, carriages, and racing; indeed, it was his family tradition. As if with fleeting excitement, a moment appears in which a sporting couple survey the field and possibly the very horse they own or on which they have bet. The rider and mount have the unvarying verve Lautrec gave such images. The strength of the primed horse, the alert tension of the equally primed jockey, are admirably fixed.

52. *At the Cirque Fernando*
1888
Oil
100.0 x 200.0cm
Art Institute of Chicago

If Degas was to take the ballet theater for his own special realm, Lautrec was just as masterfully to take the circus for his. His drawing has developed a caricaturish jauntiness of line, both economic and highly expressive. The circus's grotesque humor, its whole masquerade, was something of a "natural" for an artist of Lautrec's curious physical deformity. This justly famous work has a concentrated spirit of the circus ring. The powerful horse, the perky ballerina atop it, the thrusting action of the profiled ringmaster with his rippling whip, the accent of the dancing clown by the margin, could not be bettered for colorfully exact and vivacious atmosphere. The view has the foreshortened, or "close-up," quality of ringside seats: an effect accented by the large curving diagonal of the red and white seats themselves.

53. *Two Women Making Their Bed*
1889
Oil
61.0 x 80.0cm
Private Collection, Paris

With aristocratic dignity and self-possession, despite his crippled stuntedness, Lautrec went everywhere: to haunts high and low, to bars as well as select cafés – and to brothels. Virtually every intimate domestic scene of women in undress or negligée to be found in his works must be assumed as a brothel scene. Though it reveals unlovely, shabby types, this scene with its *triste* appreciation of something humanly rather grotesque is really sympathetic. One supposes the strange-looking little artist has been admitted freely to the confidence of these women.

54. *Woman Curling Her Hair*
1890
Oil
55.0 x 37.0cm
Musée des Augustins, Toulouse

The coarse brown board is practically a symbol for the underworld milieu of prostitutes. On it, Lautrec expertly washed his light boudoirish colors – with no idea of lending it gayety, but out of affection for its human intimacy and its essential innocence. He wished simply to record the truth of a world where he was always a welcome visitor, because he never came armed with any shade or degree of moral criticism. The image has perfect spontaneity.

55. *Gabrielle the Dancer*
1890
Oil
54.0 x 40.0cm
Musée Toulouse-Lautrec, Albi

A picture full of brisk technique that has the air of having been rapidly done. For many years Lautrec lived in Montmartre, interpreting its garish soul as a vital center of Parisian life. He probably met this music hall performer while out with his artist's equipment and asked her to pose on the spot. The characterization lacks the passionate care which he spent on many similar subjects but arrests the eye with its impromptu look.

56. *Monsieur Désiré Dihau: Bassoonist of the Opera*
1891
Oil
55.2 x 45.0cm
Musée Toulouse-Lautrec, Albi

Probably Lautrec was seeking here the conscious emulation of a man he much admired: Degas the painter of musicians and dancers. As now, the aerial viewpoint of some of Lautrec's works suggests that at moments he tried to compensate for his brief stature by placing his eyes above the subject. Not very communicative as a portrait, the image nevertheless has character, the composition is well balanced, and the shrubbery in the background is gracefully arranged without being insistent. The green and purple have become typical of the artist's outdoor palette to interpret shade.

57. *The Bed*
1892–95

Tactfully titled as it is, the subject might equally well be called *Earned Rest.* Unquestionably it is two prostitutes tucked away un-

Oil
53.0 x 70.0cm
The Louvre, Paris

der bountiful covers for the remainder of the night. Degas, too, frequented such women but for a more limited, rather abstractive aesthetic purpose. Every facet of their domestic lives intrigued and absorbed Lautrec. The color here is rather dazzling; one suspects that in the three years it took to complete the work, Lautrec thought the bed linen looked dull and proceeded to enliven it with opalescence.

58. *Woman in Black Boa*
1892
Oil
53.0 x 41.0cm
The Louvre, Paris

A wonderful example of what used to be called a speaking likeness. Literally, one can imagine the lady opening her lips the next moment to make a remark to the artist. The direct gaze at the man portraying her has just the trace of pert irony that suits the obviously made-up features of a woman whose profession is being a woman and who values her talents as a charmer. It seems the make-up is an indispensable part of her character: she would be incomplete and dismayed without it. With it, she is enchanted to become Lautrec's subject. At the same time, some grave thought, some dolorous judgment of life, secretes itself behind the wide eyes: so steadfastly, courageously looking at the world of *men* with a soupçon of mocking humor.

59. *The Englishman Warner at the Moulin Rouge*
1892
Lithograph
47.0 x 37.2cm
Musée Toulouse-Lautrec, Albi

This is a poster treatment of a subject done elsewhere in paint medium. The dark-monotoned gentleman making himself agreeable to two bedizened ladies is a technical way of bringing out the purposeful get-up of women such as frequented the famous Paris night-spot. Lautrec himself is an unfailing habitué of the place as well as a sedulous portrayer of its denizens and its atmosphere. The gay, pseudo-sinister quality of the ladies has been very cleverly interpreted.

60. *Jardin de Paris: Jane Avril*
(after the original poster)
1893
Lithograph
130.0 x 95.0cm
Musée de Toulouse-Lautrec, Albi

An image of the dancer whom Lautrec portrayed many times. Here in action on stage, she is a perfect example of the racy, somewhat cumbrous grace of popular dancing at this period. The semi-comic character of her dance deportment and style (notice the careless position of the head and the inelegant turn of the left foot) is highly veracious. Technically the poster is superb: the use of the diagonal fiddle head to form part of the thick border and the projecting angle of the music score could not be bettered for flavorous ingenuity.

61. *Loie Fuller at the Folies-Bergères*
1893
Oil
61.0 x 43.8cm
Musée Toulouse-Lautrec, Albi

Lautrec's impression of the famous performer, who danced in colored lights while waving immense veils which shrouded her, has been executed with inimitable economy. The sense of aerial thrust is portrayed by the positions of the head and bosom as well as by the vertical lines in both the swirling costume and the shadowy background. The whole, instantaneously conveyed, has a charmingly naive directness.

62. *Monsieur, Madame, and the Dog*
1893
Water Color
48.0 x 80.0cm
Musée Toulouse-Lautrec, Albi

As devout chronicler of Parisian life, Lautrec could not have missed the present rich opportunity. This monsieur and madame of the people, with household pet, may well be owners of a little café and are superbly comic without brimming over into caricature. One feels no self-consciousness in their demeanor: the working artist, whether present or not, might as well have been invisible. It may be that the couple, well known to Lautrec, represent an indelible impression he carried away with him one night and that, at once, with typical brio, he transferred rapidly to paper.

63. *Madame de Gortzikoff*
1893
Oil
75.0 x 51.0cm
Private Collection, London

Never associated with the Impressionists as a group, and coming late on the scene, Lautrec (only 29) had not held a show till this year. However, a dark, pulsing iridescence marks this generic portrait of a lady. Handsome, stylishly dressed, she is one of the many women Lautrec must have fervently admired from a distance and induced to pose for him. Not so much the unique person has been sought as certain social characteristics. Lautrec's technique distinguished itself from the large trend of Impressionism by faithfulness to outlines: a kind of meticulous drawing with the brush. At the same time, freedom of stroking is very evident.

64. *Monsieur Louis Pascal*
1893
Oil
77.0 x 53.0cm
Musée Toulouse-Lautrec, Albi

Here we have a high-toned gentleman who might have been an escort of the lady seen in the foregoing plate. Lautrec must have taken down his image (according to the leaning canvases behind him) while he was paying visits to the artist's studio. The top hat, the cane, the wing collar, the frock coat were all indispensable to formal dress at this time. The subdued blue-dominated iridescence of the whole costume is Lautrec's consistent manner of representing black (see plate 58). Notice the elegant touch of the thumb securing the cane in position while the rest of the fingers are tucked in the adjacent pocket.

65. *Two Women Sitting in a Café*
1894
Crayon and Water Color
53.8 x 37.9cm
The Louvre, Paris

The artist's facility in catching the zesty character of common Parisian life, "vulgar" in the easy-going sense, was never more apparent than in this sketch, which most probably was done on the spot. The watchfully discreet, yet exhibitionistic coquetry of "ladies of the evening" is written all over it: an irrepressible smile is the signal. Many French artists did similar café subjects, but this one is Lautrec and could be nothing but Lautrec.

66. *Woman Putting on Her Stocking*
1894
Oil
60.0 x 43.0cm
Musée Toulouse-Lautrec, Albi

We have an example of Lautrec's virtuosity in suggesting a complete visual impression and mood with minimal means. The speckled ground of the dark board itself serves for most of the woman's flesh, which elsewhere (with the exception of the rouged face) is almost pure white, as if it were in glaring light. Of course, the sanguine outlines intimate the flesh's warmth.

67. *Aristide Bruant*
1894
Lithograph
77.5 x 59.0cm
Musée Toulouse-Lautrec, Albi

The gentleman in the accepted costume of a bohemian artist was a well-known writer of popular songs during Lautrec's time. The cape's stark outline and the flat colors, of course, are derived from Japanese painting. Done with the utmost simplicity, it shows an ideal poster style and in its refined mastery suggests the dense silhouettes of Aubrey Beardsley, who was working at this period.

68. *The Tattooed Lady*
1894
Oil
62.5 x 48.0cm
Private Collection, Bern

The extraordinary lady, no doubt a professional of some kind, has inspired what is certainly one of the most acrid, ingeniously diabolic images Lautrec ever set forth. Eyes closed, painted rosebud lips patiently compressed, her large upright body inert, she is submitting to the usual ministrations of her dresser, in whose face Lautrec has concentrated a grinningly sinister mood. It may well remind us of Beardsley's more fanciful treatments of lovelier ladies being dressed by more stylish attendants.

69. *Femme de Maison*
1894
Oil
25.2 x 19.0cm
Musée Toulouse-Lautrec, Albi

Even without the explicit title, the smiling insinuation of this unsecretive profile would stamp it as one of the products of Lautrec's assiduous frequentation of brothels. The hair ribbon together with the décolletage of the chemise would alone, in fact, be sufficiently expressive. As the image of a woman, strikingly enough, it is as richly appreciative, as forthright, as some of Renoir's female busts. The artist was never more genially at one with his subject.

70. *Madame Pascal at the Piano*
1895
Oil
Musée Toulouse-Lautrec, Albi

Done in Lautrec's denser manner, when his oil paint is not so thinned, this charming and beautifully toned portrait profits accordingly. The flesh color of the lady's face, echoing with light blue, is the reverse of the light-blue wall behind her, thus forming her complement; the same is true of her hands in relation to the cool piano keys. Many of Lautrec's profiles have the look of ever so slightly averting themselves from the side of the artist's viewpoint, and such is the case here. The fact is the more significant because, as with the good-humored face before us, all the traits of personalities portrayed by Lautrec mount rhythmically in interest to the climax of the facial expression, where the chief interest, so to speak, *nests* itself. The work has much grace. Lautrec's usual long vertical stokes in the dress help the accurate feeling of a pianist's shoulders raised and poised for playing.

71. *The Two Friends*
1895
Oil
65.0 x 84.0cm
Private Collection, Zurich

Lautrec's natural candor of mind as an interested observer did not let him hesitate about portraying the lesbian relationships that were not uncommon among the inmates of brothels. The situation here should be plain enough. It is reported with the artist's inveterate alertness and basically is sympathetic. The atmosphere of indolent leisure, encouraging to amorousness, is conveyed discreetly but unmistakably, entirely without moralism or any trace of leering. The curiously disposed fingers are a very effective touch.

72. *The Female Clown Cha-U-Kao*
1895
Oil
64.0 x 49.0cm
The Louvre, Paris

This dressing-room image of a buxom performer of unusual type has much natural strength, gained largely by the informal moment and the astutely chosen angle of vision, which conceals the face's lower half and aggrandizes the body. Unquestionably, at a glance, the portrait of a particular person, it has been done by Lautrec, characteristically, to expose the bizarre *persona,* or public image, assumed by one individual. Life as a *theater* of being and action is Lautrec's dominant motif as it was that of Degas – as strictly personal as was the art of each. The design, the painting, the human inflection here are irreproachably styled.

73. *Woman at Her Toilet*
1896
Oil
67.0 x 54.0cm
The Louvre, Paris

A work inevitably suggesting comparison with Degas's treatment of the same subject. Lautrec's emphasis seems to have chosen a moment of cessation, as if the woman had paused at the artist's request. In particular evidence is Lautrec's individual manner of making oil paint look like a very rich use of watercolor. It also

Lautrec →
The Lady Clown Cha-U-Kao as Rider (Top right)
Clown, Horse, and Monkey Rider (Top left)
Entrance to the Track, Horse Saddled with Frame and Followed by Acrobat in Slippers (Bottom right)
Rehearsing on the Floor (Bottom left)

shows that, no matter how much attention is given texture and a changing opalescence of color, outline remained of indispensable importance for this artist almost to the end. The light in relation to local colors is beautifully modulated.

74. *Casual Conquest*
1896
Oil
105.0 x 67.0cm
Musée des Augustins, Toulouse

In Lautrec's day, no matter what their exact motives, gentlemen were fond of paying court to popular actresses in their dressing rooms, and as plain here, it was not the custom always to remove their top hats. This is a genre picture of Parisian life and done for amusement's sake as a notation of manners. Still, for our time, so many decades later, what must amuse us most is the lady's very bountiful proportions, so long since out of fashion. It is the coziest of moments, taken down as if in pictorial shorthand.

75. *At the Café: The Guest and the Chlorotic Cashier*
1898
Oil
81.5 x 60.0cm
Kunsthaus, Zurich

Close to the genre subject of the couple who are fixtures at a café, this is Lautrec's sharp-eyed portrayal of what is truly a café fixture: its cashier – and possibly an admirer. At any rate, it is a pungent image such as that of *Monsieur, Madame, and the Dog,* seen here in another plate. This couple, to be sure, are more on their dignity and aware that the establishment pretends to some style. The artist's sense of humor never failed to be prompted by characteristic facets of the gayer life of Paris. Alas! he knew this milieu all too well. About a year from now, he will suffer a mental collapse from alcoholism and debauchery.

76. *Monsieur Maurice Joyant (detail)*
1900
Oil
113.0 x 79.0cm
Musée Toulouse-Lautrec, Albi

The artist has recuperated from his collapse and, back at his easel, has paid his friend, dealer, and guardian angel the formal compliment of a portrait: Joyant ceaselessly watched over his painter's interests. Conceiving its subject picturesquely as a sportsman, the portrait (though quite uninspired) is doubtless a good likeness. The sail beyond denotes that Joyant loved boating; in fact, he owned a yacht on which he wanted Lautrec to rest by taking a trip. But nothing could now save this artist, doomed to his addictions.

77. *Portrait of a Woman*
1900
Oil
89.5 x 80.5cm
Ohara Art Gallery, Kurashiki, Japan

One is induced to think, from this well-fleshed lady doubtless accustomed to a life of ease, that Lautrec has been studying Renoir's women with a certain admiration. She seems to have the type of face that attracted Lautrec, yet there is a lack of sharp focus in the way she has been portrayed, even a sort of indecisiveness in the

← *Chocolate Dancing in the Bar d'Achille*

drawing; for example, about the bosom. Evidently, it was not easy for the artist to do precisely what he seems to have tried to do here: abandon the sovereignty of his outlines and somewhat, too, his savor of character. All the same, his women have lost neither their femininity nor their appeal.

78. *The Milliner*
1900
Oil
61.0 x 49.3cm
Musée Toulouse-Lautrec, Albi

Surely this is a somewhat milder Lautrec than the social commentator or the character portraitist. The pretty young woman's face, while it has a curl of lip typical of Lautrec's women, seems no more important than her piled hair or her fancy blouse. It is clear, too, that the painter has been moved to let illuminated contour replace the governing linear quality that used to characterize his style. The work remains, like the subject, a very pretty piece, its main plastic interest being the shape of the lady's luminous form seen against her dark surroundings.

79. *Portrait of André Rivoire*
1901
Oil
57.5 x 46.0cm
Musée du Petit-Palais, Paris

Surely, in this very late work, it is plain that the artist had decided, *à l'Impressioniste,* to play with texture less systematically, to use more impasto and let the lighted plane supersede the outline. Indeed, there is an air of experimentality about it, a kind of searching aspect, which one would not expect from a craftsman of Lautrec's masterly attainments. But this was the year of his death. His amazingly prolific career would be over at the age of thirty-seven.

EDGAR DEGAS

1834	Edgar Degas born in Paris on July 19. The father's family was Breton, but had left France during the Revolution and settled in Naples. The mother's family had also left France during the Revolution and settled in New Orleans. The family name was "de Gas" but Degas himself changed the form.
1845–52	At school, at the Lycée Louis le Grand.
1852–54	Begins to study art on full-time basis, under Barrias and Lamothe.
1854–59	Regular visits to Italy, where he studies Renaissance and ancient art.
1859	In April, takes a studio in the rue Madam, Paris, and concentrates on portraiture and historical subjects.
1865–70	Contributes regularly to the official Salon. By 1865, However, he has already met Whistler, Fantin Latour, Renoir, Manet and Sisley.
1870	Serves in the Franco-Prussian war. By this date, he is already interested in such "modern" subjects as the theater and horses and riders.
1872–73	Visits his brothers in New Orleans and paints several pictures there.
1874	Contributes to the first Impressionist Exhibition in Paris (as he will to all the others with the exception of the 1882 show).
1880	Visit to Spain.
1886	Contributes to the last of the Impressionist Exhibitions. After this date ceases to send his work to public exhibitions, though they are shown commercially by Durand-Ruel, the dealer. By this date, Degas is working more and more in pastel.
1889	Visits Spain with the painter Boldini.
1905	Exhibition of Impressionists organized by Durand-Ruel at the Grafton Galleries in London. The *Times* critic singles out Degas for attack.
1911	Becomes an Honorary Member of the Royal Scottish Academy.
1912	By this date Degas has become famous and his works relatively popular. La Danseuse à la Barre (New York, Metropolitan Museum), in fact, fetches about $100,000 (450,000 francs) at auction.
1917	September 27. Dies in Paris, and is buried in the family tomb at the Montmartre cemetery.

HENRI DE TOULOUSE-LAUTREC

1864	November 24, Henri-Marie-Raymond de Toulouse-Lautrec Monfa born in the Hotel du Bosc, the family house at Albi. His father was Count Alphose and his mother, a first cousin of her husband's, Adele Tapié de Cèleyran.
1872	The family moves to Paris, where Henri goes to school at the Lycée Fontanes. Here he meets Maurice Joyant, who was to remain one of his most devoted friends.
1878	The family returns to Albi, where Henri continues his education with his mother. He falls on a slippery floor and breaks his left leg.
1879	Lautrec now breaks his right femur; he remains an invalid and is obliged to give up his favorite sports, riding and shooting.
1881	His formal education ceases when he passes the first part of his baccalaureate. Takes his first formal drawing lessons with Renè Princeteau, an animal painter.
1882	On Princeteau's advice, he enrolls in Bonnat's studio in Paris, but only stays there a short time because Bonnat decides to abandon teaching. Continues his studies under Cormon.
1880s	Becomes increasingly tied to Montmartre, where he finds his subjects, models, friends and mistresses. Becomes friendly (1885) with the singer Bruant, and first shows his paintings in public on the walls of Bruant's cabaret, "Le Mirliton."
1887	From 1887 Lautrec's work is widely shown in group exhibitions: the Société des Vingt (Paris and Brussels), the Salon des Indépendants, the Cercle Volney, the Arts Liberaux, etc. Lautrec also works for periodicals, such as *Rire, Figaro Illustré, Courrier Français* and *Paris Illustré.*
1891	Makes his first lithographic print with a poster for the Moulin Rouge. During the early 1890s, paints many pictures of the dance halls and of the stars who appeared there. Also begins to work in brothels, often living in them for days on end.
1893	Holds his first important exhibition with Charles Maurin at the Boussod-Valadon Gallery in Paris.
1894	Visits London with Maurice Joyant. Publishes an album of his lithographs devoted to the diseuse Yvette Guilbert.

1899 At the end of February, he suffers a complete collapse and is taken to a sanatorium at Neuilly, where he remains until May. While undergoing treatment, he makes a series of drawings from memory of circus subjects. After leaving the sanatorium, he begins painting again. Stays at le Grotoy, le Havre, Arcachon, Bordeaux.

1901 Attempts to resume his old way of life, but even though only in his mid-thirties, whoring and drinking have taken their toll. In August, he arrives at Malromé to visit his mother. On September 9 he dies.

About the author: Parker Tyler has written widely on art for more than twenty years. He has appeared frequently in *The Magazine of Art, The American Artist, Arts Digest,* and *Art News* (of which he was editorial associate, 1954-1958) and was managing editor of *Art News Annual* for two years. He is the author of *The Divine Comedy of Pavel Tchelitchew* (1967), *Florine Stettheimer: A Life in Art,* a monograph on Conrad Marca-Relli, three books of verse, books of film criticism, and a book of literary essays. His poetry is represented in important anthologies, and his essays on the film appear in literary and film anthologies. He received a citation from *The Nation* for his book *Chaplin* (1948) and from *The New Republic* for his play *The Screen.*

Photographed by André Held (plate 7,34) Toshio Ushiyama (19,27) René Roland (37,38) Photographie Giraudon (1,2,3,4,5,6,8,9,10,11,12, 13,14,15,16,17,18,20,21,22,23,24,25,26,28,29,30,31,32,33,35,36,40,41,42,43,44,45,46,47,48,49,50,51,52,53,54,55,56, 57,58,59,60,61,62,63,64,65,66,67,68,69,70,71,72,73,74,75,76,78,79) Zauho Press (39,77)

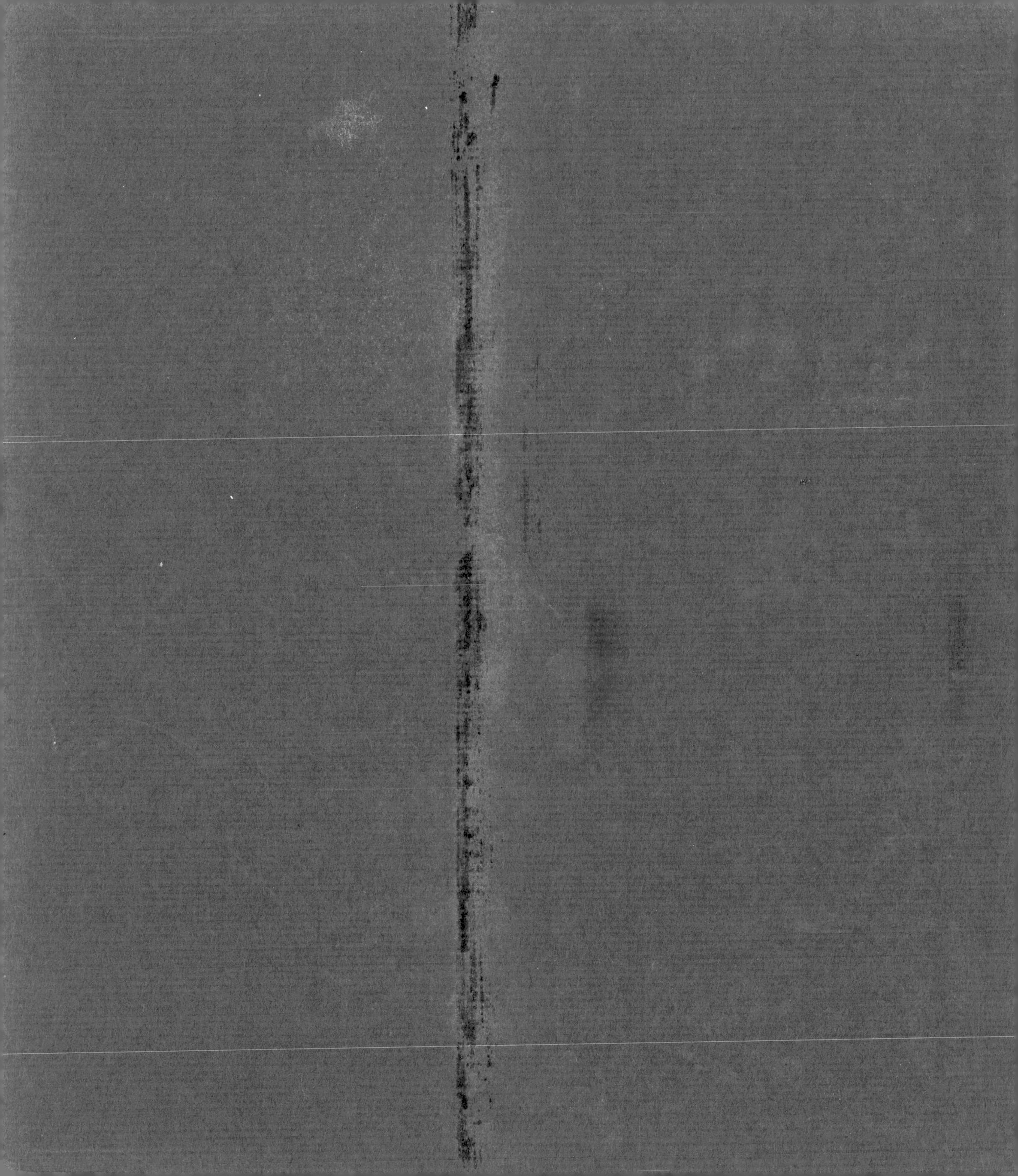